THE THREE ROOTS

Identifying and Overcoming FEAR,
PRIDE, and IGNORANCE

RUDOLPH BRISCOE

Book Cover Design by HCP Book Publishing

ISBN: 978-976-96174-0-7 (paperback)

978-976-96174-1-4 (eBook)

Dedication

To Carole, my Queen

To Ruth-Ann, Karo-Lee, and Noellene—my Princesses.
They are my inspiration.

ENdorSeMeNtS

This is a timely writing on an important subject that affects all of us negatively—the lack of knowledge about this phenomenon called Fear. We continue to suffer, but this book has turned on a floodlight in this area, so no one needs to suffer in the dark anymore because of fear and pride. Good work, Rev. Briscoe. This is a must-read for everyone who wants to be free from the prison of fear, pride, or ignorance.

~ *Min. Michael McLean, Fellowship Tabernacle, Kingston, Jamaica.*

I recommend this book for anyone who is ready for self-examination and for those who are searching for healing remedies to grow in every arena of your life, whether professional, spiritual, and/or personal.

~ *David Aaron Johnson, Pastor, Professor, and Apostle of Reconciliation in Seattle, Washington, U.S.A.*

Preface

Three roots to the problems of humanity is not a new concept, as the Buddhists have had a similar idea for ages. However, instead of fear, pride, and ignorance, they speak of anger/hate, greed, and ignorance. It is clear that these all relate and feed into each other and therefore must be considered and examined to break free and avoid the accompanying pitfalls.

Journey with us as we look at these roots and how they affect us and how we can manage and overcome them and their adverse effects. Being deceived in thinking that we are never susceptible to any of these is to play into the hands of the enemy, who is planning to keep us bound.

It does not matter your religion or whether you have a religion— you were never created to be in bondage to anything negative. You shall know the truth, and the truth shall set you free!

Foreword

The story is told of a prisoner of war who was captured by enemies known to be vicious. At his trial, he was given two choices, *"You can either go through this door (a door the judge pointed to) and be a free man, or you can face the firing squad."* Fear gripped him so tight because of the reputation of his captors that he chose the firing squad. It turned out that the first option was a true offer. He missed it because he was fearful of an option he knew nothing about.

That happens to a lot of us as we navigate life's treacherous paths. Many of us are fearful, obnoxiously proud, and sometimes fail to realize that we don't know some things that we should know. If more of us face our fears, we would surprise ourselves with additional achievements on top of what we have accomplished so far. Many of our relationships would improve, and more people would find us 'nice' to be near. We would even conquer some mountains that we thought were impossible to climb.

I have known Rudolph for more than thirty years. He has functioned in many capacities: a teacher, insurance salesman, student leader, pastor, and counselor. The volume and variety of his interactions with a wide cross-section of people have given him the insight into the inner workings of people's core attitudes that cause success or failure in their lives.

There will be pointed questions in this book for you to answer for yourself, as I have had to do, especially in the section on fear. Why haven't I attempted some things that are in my heart and I believe to be right? It will cause you to examine your motives and ask yourself, *"Am I pretending to know what I don't know sufficient of?"*

We can all eradicate The Three Roots of Fear, Pride, and Ignorance, as we allow the words of this book to get inside of us and behind the walls that we have erected to continue our charades.

Buy two copies of this book; one for you and another for your best friend.

Morton (Steve) Waugh
Author of *Smart Parents' Children Finish Well:*
Are You Even Listening?

TabLe oF CoNteNtS

Introduction

God wants each of us to be successful in this life. We were created for success and not failure. But there are three main roots to most of the problems we encounter on our journey. We wrestle not against flesh and blood, but God created the natural things for us to better understand the spiritual, the spiritual being more real than the natural. Hence, the analogy of the natural tree being brought forth from a seed sown and germinating to producing a 'radicle,' then the 'plumule,' then branches and fruits.

Roots run deep and sometimes hold strong and stubborn in the soil. I remember seeing some workmen trying to dislodge a tree trunk from a public property. They tried digging around the tree trunk and then pulling the trunk out with a van and then a backhoe from a tractor but to no avail. One guy even mentioned he had seen a backhoe damaged trying to do the same thing. The roots of a tree were meant to harness that tree in the ground and make it strong to withstand assault but also to take nutrients from the soil around it for the rest of the tree.

These negative roots are FEAR, PRIDE, and IGNORANCE, which will hold us firmly in their grip for 'fear' of losing us to any other 'competition.' They will also feed us toward growth and development in the direction they want us to go. However, is that the direction we were created to go in? The purpose God has for us is better, by far; to have good success, to be fruitful and multiply, producing righteous seed for His glory.

Then, there are also the positive seeds that were sown and will grow to counteract the negative ones; they are FAITH, CONFIDENCE, and HOPE. These will help us fulfill our purpose, if we focus on getting them.

"If the root is holy, so are the branches and the root support the whole tree" (paraphrase, **Romans 11:16-18).**

My intention is to help the reader identify any one or combinations of these negative roots and help you use them in a positive way.

> *"But as for you, you meant evil against me; but God meant it for your good," (Genesis 50:20a).*

Identifying and using your nagative roots in a positive way will result in more meaningful activities, and achievement of one's goals and, as Joyce Meyer puts it, *"Enjoying everyday life!"*

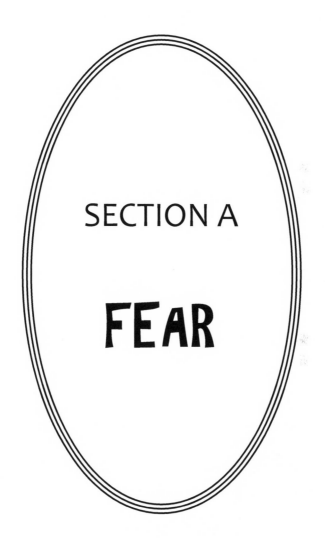

SECTION A

FEAR

For God has not given us a spirit of fear, but of power and of love and of a sound mind.

(2 Timothy 1:7 – NKJV)

CHAPTER ONE

IS IT FEAR, OR NOT?

The most common and most easily identified of the three roots is **fear,** and it exposes us to other negative seeds. Fear can be debilitating and crippling in some instances. Chronic fear can even affect one's health and productivity at work or school. Fear can be a good warning signal to us at times, but other times, unwarranted fear can be a great nuisance if not dealt with properly. Dr. Gary Collins states, *"Anxiety, stress, fear, phobia, tension – technically these words have different meanings, but they are used interchangeably to describe one of this century's most common problems."* [1]

The first mention of fear in the Bible is found in **Genesis 3:10**:

"So he said, "I heard Your voice in the garden, and I was afraid because I was naked; and I hid myself."

Adam was suddenly afraid and possibly did not understand why at the time. He must have been afraid of being found out after having done wrong or afraid of whatever consequences would be meted out to him. He may also have been afraid of being seen naked, exposed, and without covering. Fear is the primary tool of the enemy of our souls, Satan himself. Even in the natural, other people may use fear to their advantage against us, such as tyrants, robbers, rapists, abusers, and gang members.

We have been taught by many experts to downplay fear, that it is a normal human emotion we all must live with. While this is true, we don't all respond the same way, and those affected the most are the ones needing the intervention the most. Many people, while not troubled by fear, seem to almost ridicule those who are. People who are troubled by fear may not be able to live a normal life without the help of someone else who is concerned about them.

Some people may acknowledge fear in their lives while others may realize that they have a block regarding certain activities, but don't understand why they will not proceed with the desired action. People with *acrophobia* (fear of height) or *claustrophobia* (fear of being in enclosed spaces), may readily admit their fears, but some other types of fear may not be so easily identified.

Other people may admit they are afraid but don't know why they are afraid.

In many places in Scripture, God encourages us to "fear not" or "be not afraid," for example, *Joshua 1:8, Isaiah 41:10, Matthew 17:7,* and all throughout the Gospels. Fear can also be hidden in our lives without us realizing it, and some fears can be disguised as something else. We will go into more detail later as we look more closely at this root.

Possible sources or seeds of fear can be from words spoken by our parents or things they may have done to us as children. Others may be word-pictures picked up from just about anywhere, such as dreams, movies, traumatic events, and so on. The fears we experience may have come from anywhere, but one thing is sure—we all have to deal with some fear or another.

Our instincts or intuition will draw on a sense of fear to warn us when there is pending danger. It is the negative impact that is not desirable. How do we respond when we become afraid?

TYPES OF FEAR

Fear of FAILURE often results from a loss, poverty-stricken situations, broken heartedness, etc. This often leads to selfishness, aloneness, unwillingness to take risks, love of money, and a miserly or mean attitude.

Derrick Johnson from Ipswich Town lost at love when he was in high school. Derrick never had a girlfriend all through college and seemed doomed to never getting married. One day he saw a girl named Debbie at work who he liked. They talked and laughed and even had lunch together, and then one day the conversation got around to going steady and getting serious. Derrick found every excuse there was to never get close to Debbie again. Of course, he was educated and accomplished and knew his way around with women, but Derrick was afraid of making any commitment because he was afraid to fail again!

Many people have this type of fear disguised as something else, such as false humility, patience, or carefulness. None of these in their masking roles will ever allow the person to realize their dreams.

Fear of SUCCESS usually results from seeing others not handling success well and not wanting the same to happen to you. Another factor is being unsure of the changes that would result, the changes to one's routine and privacy, the limelight, the pressure, the demands, and maybe the stress related to keeping that success. As a result, one does not try to accomplish that which may make one successful and thereby make seemingly reasonable or even pathetic excuses.

Jake Turner was good at mathematics and always seemed to do exceptionally well, even when he missed classes; he didn't seem to study at all. A mathematics competition came up that offered a huge cash prize, a new car, and a trip to Europe! Most people would be excited to enter such a competition, especially if they stand a chance, but not Jake. His excuses for not entering were all philosophical and of deep rationalizations, but, really, Jake was afraid. He was fearful that if he won, he would not know what to do with himself and all the fuss that came with it.

Fear of PEOPLE may result from past experiences but can also come from the projection of an image you have of that person or someone they remind you of. The Bible says it this way, *"Do not be afraid of their faces,"* *(Jeremiah 1:8).* This may be due to feeling shame, rejection, or a sense that they are superior in physical strength, intelligence, or skill. This type of fear sometimes results in one lying to avoid people or staying away from activities that would involve people that one thinks would put them in competition.

Leesa Springer is a beautiful well-to-do music teacher from Missouri who is quite confident in her abilities. However, one day she saw a young cellist who played as a guest performer from another church. She played like a born genius. Leesa is used to being the ace musician and was seldom equaled or surpassed in skills, but now she feels quite awkward being up-scaled by such a young talent. Uncharacteristically, she became nervous and was afraid to play any of her pieces that evening.

Fear of DEATH or DANGER, for example, accidents, robberies, and natural disasters, is a type of fear that can be just as irrational as all the others but can be used for our advantage, if the energy is funneled into prevention and preparation activities or quick response activities in case something happens.

Ainsworth Jenkins has been deathly afraid of outings ever since his older brother died in a car accident. All this changed when Ainsworth learned CPR (cardio-pulmonary resuscitation), took swimming lessons and learned defensive driving. This does not work for everyone, but it did for Ainsworth.

Fear of REJECTION is another common fear, yet not easily identified, primarily by its victim. Though this may be found in many scenarios, a familiar place for this is in relationship dynamics. Many children and women fall prey to this type of fear, but a lot of men are affected in their sex life because of fear of rejection.

Suzan Fields is a beautiful and appealing woman, and one would think she is secure in her marriage to her husband, Bobby. However, he complains about her tentativeness regarding sexual intercourse. It never occurred to him that his beautiful career woman was afraid of rejection, and as a result, seldom initiated sexual contact with him. This affected their marriage, as Bobby was often tempted to entertain the many women who throw themselves at him. Most men enjoy a woman who is not afraid of taking it to him, the kind of woman who is not afraid to turn him on.

Fear of CRITICISM is a common fear and is also one of the most destructive in that many dreams and aspirations have been aborted because of it. While it seems similar to the fear of Rejection, it is not the same. Fear of criticism makes you most concerned about what someone may say or think about you and your actions, irrespective of consequential rejection. Their possible opinion about us freezes us.

> Jason is keen in his studies and has an inquiring mind, but I found out that he could have been far more advanced in his work if he was not so afraid to say what he was thinking. Many times, Jason has an idea or has a question but refuses to say anything at the time until some key people have left the room. He is not afraid of the people, but subconsciously afraid of what anyone else may say in response. I say 'anyone else' because he is not bothered by the opinions of those who are close to him. We are his friends and, after all, friends 'rib' each other.

Many people are afraid of the DARK, whether because they are superstitious or they just like to see what is around them. While this is understandable, to a certain extent, it is cause for concern when it becomes chronic, for example:

> Verland is a man from the country, and he loves the outdoors. He involves himself in a lot of activities, and he is fun loving. I found, however, that though he is a big man, he never ventures into dark areas alone. He avoids dark areas, even to the detriment of his health. He refuses to go to a restroom in another building because of the dark, preferring to 'hold it' until morning.

The fear of certain ANIMALS may also seem acceptable. While one will not be naïve and place one's self in unnecessary danger, the Bible did state that God would put the fear of man on all animals (**Genesis 9:2).** Some dogs have been trained to attack strangers, and one should not believe they will not attack just because of this verse. Bible teacher Andrew Wommack tells the story of a man who jogged in the mornings. On one such morning, a neighbor's Doberman got loose. The man was seen running from the dog in one direction and then seen chasing the dog in the opposite direction. After remembering and believing this Bible verse, there was a role reversal between man and dog. Some people are terrified of a cockroach, a mouse, or a tiny lizard, notwithstanding that most of these animals are terrified themselves and are seeking to get away from a human as quickly as possible.

Many types of fears exist, and more are discovered as time progresses. The important thing is to own and acknowledge your fears, and then you can respond more positively rather than continue to be a victim, knowingly or not. In his book, *The Gift of Fear*, De Becker states *"Most people are great victims because they ignore their fears and survival signals rather than facing them and converting retreat to advance."*[2]

Sometimes, fear can be so obvious, but we may feel too ashamed to admit it. One victim said it was so real to her it was *"like an animal hiding within her."*

Then there is '**Islamophobia**,' where people are traumatized by seeing someone wearing a 'hijab' or 'burqa' because of the many instances of suicide bombers in the news. This may be irrational to some people, but real to others. Living in constant fear at periods of one's life can rob us of a meaningful life.

The same goes for '**homophobia**,' where just the hint of a homosexual tendency causes some people to be visibly shaken and fearful. One may not be sure how to respond to such a person. A conversation could be awkward or frankly impossible for this person. While that may be so, they may just have missed an important moment in their existence because they could not function normally.

Can you think of anyone you know who acts like any of those mentioned above? Do you recognize any of these fears in your own life? We all have fears; we all experience them at one time or another, but do we acknowledge them? Do we ignore them, thinking that they will just go away, or do we have to live with them?

Many try to co-exist peacefully and do the best they can, but others find that their fear grows to unbearable proportions. Our aim is to help you first to identify and acknowledge the fears that hinder you and then to be able to respond to them differently where necessary.

In the next chapter, we will look at some cases of chronic fear and see what can happen when fear sets in deeply inside us and affects us badly. Fear has driven people to certain mental illnesses as well as to suicide. Early intervention is therefore necessary before symptoms of critical levels phobia and paranoia sets in.

CHAPTER TWO

HAS IT BORNE FRUIT?

As fear grows in one's life, it becomes a part of the person, a fixture that attaches itself. This brings about a predictable feeling or attitude. One becomes withdrawn easily and develops feelings of disappointment, discouragement, and sometimes depression. The bully syndrome or show-off attitude is often used to mask these feelings. A sense of false security is used to protect one from the real world unknowingly. Sometimes one finds an area he or she is better in than someone else and uses that area as a defense shield from venturing into any other area. One may sometimes lie to hide feelings of doubt and inferiority, which may develop into cynicism, hate, and selfishness.

No one can pretend all the time—it can be tiring. Those who are close to us, and know us well, can see the leaves and the branches of our fears. They see them hanging off us and waving at times as the wind of everyday life blows at them. They become almost impossible to miss once one gets to know us. Fear, when it sets in, often masks itself as shyness. People who usually seem shy at times are locked down with fear, but most times we all think it is normal. Once we accept constant shyness as normal, it can grow into a stronghold that will become more difficult to break free of later.

In the church, for instance, people will not readily admit to their fears because it is not spiritual. This causes a lot of people in the church to live in fear almost all their lives, while masking it with false humility, spirituality, and self-righteousness, often pointing at another person's flaws to deflect from their own problems. This means there can be such a thing as a spiritual bully in the church.

When people harbor fear in their life for an inordinately long period without any intervention, this results in long-term, seemingly permanent conditions. When, for instance, there is a constant cycle of failure, an underlying root triggers this recurring result. As stated in the book, *No Longer a Victim*, "*Its victims usually realize its irrationality, but are helpless to halt its control over their lives.*" [3]

Recurring failure can be a fruit of the fear of failure mentioned earlier and, if not addressed, may continue unchecked for many years. If you are repeatedly failing, maybe fear is working in your life. Job says:

> *"For the thing I greatly feared has come upon me, and what I dreaded has happened to me." (**Job 3:25**).*

St. Luke 21:25-36 speaks about an increase of fear in the last days: *"Men's hearts failing them for fear ..."*

Another resultant fruit of fear is *violence*. Many times, one who displays a pattern of violence in their lives does so unknowingly due to fear. This may just be their way of coping with their personal challenges. This could also be a great source of distraction from a situation that shows them up in one area. The so-called bully is a personality that is often hiding one type of fear or another and helping to identify that fear or other emotional issues can prevent a long life of violence and confusion.

Identifying fear, whether from the root, branch, or fruit, is essential in learning to live a meaningful and productive life.

Franklyn Josephs is an electrician who works well and is helpful not only to the clients but also his supervisor and his fellow employees. One of his co-workers argued profusely with Franklyn one day. Apparently, Franklyn had lent out one of his tools to a senior worker, and this seemed to be happening more frequently than not.

They had a pressuring assignment and could not complete it on the day in question because he had lent out his tool yet again. His co-worker argued that Franklyn was afraid of the guy and that was why he always lent his tool to him even though he knew he might need it. This was one such day, and his co-worker was incensed, saying, *"We are having this problem because you are afraid him, afraid to ask the man for your tool. You know you need it!"* Franklin replied rather sheepishly that he had reminded the man that he would need it urgently today but here they were again as many times before. He further justified his behavior by saying he was not afraid of him, but only respects him.

I feel for Franklyn. People like him are afraid of certain people and will excuse it rather than admit it. He now has a habit of doing this when he is afraid of someone, rather than stand up to them. We must understand that people who like to abuse other people have a knack for finding the fearful. They thrive on using those people who will let them. Allowing your fears to ruin your life will become an accepted position and set a pattern of behavior.

It is interesting that Franklyn uses the excuse of *respect* because the word *fear* as used in the Bible can also mean *respect, reverence,* and *awe* of God instead of 'being afraid of.' This is one reason

fear is just as much a problem in the church as it is outside of the church. Being afraid of God sets the tone for fear to run rampant in the life of the believer who does not know any better. Then they learn to be afraid of most authority figures, instead of respecting them without fear. In many churches, questioning someone in authority is deemed out of order. This makes leaders unaccountable in some respects and leads to many other problematic issues.

Sunshine is beautiful and talented but has a history of being in abusive relationships. Her baby's father beats her so badly she cannot keep a job due to time lost from work. She manages to move on to another relationship eventually, but the cycle continues. She escapes to another state far away but still lives in fear that he might track her down and hurt her. How can such a lovely, talented, beautiful person suffer so much at the hands of a mere mortal? The answer is fear, and once it sets in, it triggers a way of life for the victim that renders them powerless to fight their abuser in a meaningful way. They lack the will to contest in any form, sometimes physically, legally, mentally, or even morally. These victims blame themselves most of the time and even feel sorry for the abuser.

Now, many people don't have the experiences of Franklyn or Sunshine, but they may have some instances that resemble these. That is because though there is fear, it has not reached the stage where it affects their daily lifestyle, but it can one day.

Some people are unwilling to leave the safety of their homes because of fear. They become reclusive, yet they are intelligent and full of potential. People purchase firearms because of fear, which may also put them in greater danger since they now become a target for thieves who believe they now have greater treasures to protect or they just want to steal the firearm itself.

I would like to revisit some types of fear here, as well as introduce a few more. **Fear of the DARK** can so cripple a person that they are afraid to do simple things such as sleep, drive alone, or go to the bathroom alone. When fear has so gripped you, it has become irrational and unwarranted. At this point, one needs to seek intervention.

Another fruit of fear has produced the boom in the security industry; many people are fortified in their home with many additions to protect them from intruders. This is because so many people are plagued by the **fear of DEATH** or fear of being robbed. Anything to deal with death, blood, or weapons is enough to cause some people to freak out nowadays. The security industry, as well as the advertising industry, use this to their advantage, and we see the adverts looking like a mini-movie with all the suspense and drama to get us to purchase more gadgets and upgrade our service contracts.

I know a business leader who lost the company he founded after many years because he was afraid of the CRITICISM of people he brought with him from the old company. He needed to give his senior manager the authority to hold these people accountable for their work, but, instead, he allowed the company to go under. I am sure he regrets that to this day, but, instead of taking responsibility, he placed the blame somewhere else.

Fear of DEATH, fear of WATER, and AGORAPHOBIA—the fear of wide open spaces—can become counterproductive. Most times it seems the fear has taken on a life of its own and someone or something else is controlling the person. These are signs that one may need biblical counseling because the problem may be beyond traditional medicine or therapy. These in their chronic forms can hinder a person from performing key functions and therefore curtail one's outstanding performance and, by extension, their career.

My earliest recollection of death was the demise of the matriarch in the house I was staying at the time. I was about three years old. "Mammy," as she was affectionately called, was jovial, and we played all the time. So when she passed, I obviously missed her. This was back in the 'country' environment where the dead were often prepared for burial at the family homes. I remember going up to the casket and viewing the body but was never afraid because "Mammy" was always friendly to me. I found out later that others were scared of viewing the body and I wondered why.

I also remember wondering, *"What if my mother should die?"* This happened when I was about ten or eleven years old. I cannot think of any particular reason this thought came to me, but I remember thinking through the possibility and what that would mean.

This caused me to plan what I would do to continue life after my mother was gone even as a young child. I knew how to do the things my mother did and how to handle her financial affairs. I could wash, cook, and clean and I worked it all out. I faced the fear of the possible death of my mother and won.

People have literally lost their lives due to fear. Some have committed suicide because of a mental illness arising from fear and anxiety. Others may have acted violently due to an unwarranted fear in some instances, and some people end up harming themselves while trying to flee from someone or something they believe will harm them. People do things they do not want to do or perhaps find out that they did things they never thought they would have done, all because of fear. This emotion can be powerful. Many people rule with fear because it is a great motivator. Spouses, bosses, gang leaders, rulers, parents, and many people use fear as an integral part of their life.

Many people cannot get a decent night's sleep because of fear. Most of us can't imagine that someone would live for years without adequate sleep because of fear, yet it happens. Many people are accustomed to having nightmares every night without fail. If they miss one night, they look out for the next episode with absolute certainty.

People who display certain behaviors have made another step toward chronic, unwarranted fear, also called phobias.

Consider people who are always looking around them, glancing at the doors seemingly unnecessarily, exhibiting uncalled-for nervousness—including sweaty palms and trembling. Some people refuse to go outside but stay indoors all day for weeks or they hyperventilate when there is an onset of their fear. Science has come up with several names for extreme conditions, such as **paranoia** and **Sudden Panic Syndrome**. [4]

CHAPTER THREE

DON'T LET FEAR STOP YOU!

*The Bible states in **2 Timothy 1:7**, "For God has not given us a spirit of fear, but of power and of love and of a sound mind."*

"Perfect love casts out all fear" (1 John 4:18) and "faith worketh by love" (Galations 5:6). It is the love God has for us that helps us. When we receive and believe it; it gives us the confidence to fight.

God never intended for us to live in fear but to master it in exercising our power, loving others, and being self-controlled in our daily activities—never driven about by unknown forces.

Fear can become a spiritual stronghold in one's life, but praise be to our God, this can be broken. One can become free from the prison of fear and be able once again to function normally.

COURAGE

While fleeing because of fear can save a person's life, most times fear allows the perpetrator of that fear to overtake and overpower their victim. Courage, on the other hand, allows a person to respond in a productive way, despite the fear. It takes courage to face one's fear and decide not to let fear conquer you. Fear will win over you if you give in and give up. Decide to beat it! There is always a way, no matter how difficult it seems now. Where there is a will, there is a way. **Matthew 14:27** reads: *"But immediately Jesus spoke to them, saying, "Be of good cheer! It is I; do not be afraid."*

Decide to face your fears once and for all. This is called **courage.** Courage is deciding to act, despite the fear. Courage provokes us to take the right action although we are afraid. We would not need courage if there were no fear at all. Fear has produced courage in us when we decide not to give in.

"The only thing we have to fear is fear itself" comes from the 1933 presidential inauguration speech by President Franklin Delano Roosevelt. *"He fell ill to a severe case of polio. The dark days that followed left him in twisted physical pain. But a determined Roosevelt, whose career many observers thought was over, summoned*

*the depths of his personal courage and regained the use of his hands
and learned to walk with braces. During his convalescence, a fear of
fire tormented Roosevelt – that he would be trapped in a burning
building. His life, already devastated, who would blame him if he
spent the rest of his days wallowing in self-pity? Instead, he struggled
to overcome his disability and conquer fear."* [5]

Fear can be properly managed and used to fuel our passions instead
of killing our dreams and aspirations. As we saw earlier, fear can be
an essential warning to us of impending danger if we pay attention
rather than disregard it. Fear can be measured and rechanneled in
another direction. Emotional energy need not be wasted.

The first step, of course, is acknowledging that something is
not right. Admitting the need for help is a significant step in
obtaining a solution to any problem. Otherwise, one will be
unlikely to get help. As the old saying goes: *"You can lead a horse
to water, but you cannot make him drink it."*

CALLING

Fear will try to prevent us from moving into our purpose or
calling. Many people tell of the great challenges of fear before
finding success in a particular area of their life. Confronting your
fears is also one of the keys to being successful and finding the
area you were made to function in.

Some of us have found our niche in life, but fear can cause us
to miss opportunities, even while we are in our zone of calling.

Apostle Paul, in **Acts 28,** was bitten by a deadly and poisonous snake after being shipwrecked on an island. If Paul was so afraid of snakes that he could not function, he would have missed a great opportunity to minister there. He led a revival meeting and healed a sick man by the power of God.

Moses was called to deliver the people of Israel. Imagine being caught between the Red Sea and Pharaoh's army. The Bible says the people were filled with fear, and I am sure Moses was not peacefully happy either. God told Moses to tell the people to go forward. He gave Moses the way out and will do the same for you. He will do it for you and your family, for you and your ministry or company. He will do it for you.

FAITH

Most Bible-believing church attendees say faith is the opposite of fear but it is not. The opposite of fear is peace. However, we get that peace through faith in God and His Word. So we must start with what God has said about us.

Even if you are not a born-again Christian, the Word of God is true, no matter who you are.

Breaking free from fear may or may not require a laying on of hands deliverance sessions. Some people have been delivered (that is set free) from a lot of things just by applying the Word of God.

Many people have been set free by applying *2 Timothy 1:7* or *Genesis 9:2*.

Exercising faith in God makes you able to do things that fear has prevented you from doing in the past. Philippians 4:13 says: *"I can do all things through Christ who strengthens me."*

Faith comes from the Word of God, and we all have faith. Now that is good news.

"So then faith comes by hearing, and hearing by the word of God." *(Romans 10:17)*. So you can build your faith by using the Word of God. Your faith in God, when exercised, will let you do things that you were once afraid to do.

If you believe you can, you will, but that is not just a mental agreement to what you heard or read. It is actually doing that which confirms what you believe. James says, *"But someone will say, "You have faith, and I have works." Show me your faith without your works, and I will show you my faith by my works. You believe that there is one God. You do well. Even the demons believe— and tremble!" (James 2:18-19)*.

Faith says **"I can."** Fear says "I better not."

When I was in primary school, I was threatened by one of my classmates. He constantly threatened to beat me up after class. When school was over that day, I ran as fast as I could to get away from him. He chased me with all he had in him; it seems he was set to kill me or something. But I asked myself, *"Why am I running from this guy?"* I didn't have a good response, and I had never fought before in my life. I decided to face him, and, in mid-chase, I abruptly came to a stop halfway up the side of a wall and spun around to face Devon. He was utterly terrified, and I gave chase. I was in third grade at the time, and I became the class hero, getting the attention of all the girls as well. I learned that most bullies were counting on you being afraid of them. Devon became a good friend after that day.

> *God told Isaiah "and say to him: 'Take heed, and be quiet; do not fear or be fainthearted for these two stubs of smoking firebrands, for the fierce anger of Rezin and Syria, and the son of Remaliah." (Isaiah 7:4).*

Do not feed your fears by giving into them. Focus feeds fear just as it does faith. Focus on faith and your faith will be fed and give you the strength to respond positively to fear. In the Bible, Caleb and Joshua did not give into their fears as the other spies did. They faced their fears and made the right decision to get the better of their fears. These two came back with a positive report on the situation, while the other spies spread fear among the people.

Unhealthy fear of God is not faith. The Bible speaks of 'fearing God' to mean having reverential respect for God and who He is. Being afraid of God is contradictory to the fact that God himself tells you not to be afraid. Fearing God and not man speaks to seeing the power of God as being so insurmountably greater than the power of any man. Knowing the 'terror of God' is wisdom, understanding 'the wrath of God' is scriptural, but knowing God also means we know His love, grace, and mercy. Knowing who God is, makes us respect Him to the maximum and not trifle with His grace. David chose judgment at the hand of God, than at the hands of men when he was found guilty because He knew God (*2 Samuel 24:14*).

Fear has also been used to minimize the Christian's faith. In today's post-modern society, it is most commonly seen in our response to socio-political tensions. For example, tolerance, rights, and peaceful co-existence have been unfairly used terms in describing the relations of the church to our social ills. Due to the fear of being labeled, bullied, or getting into contentious arguments and numerous wars, some parts of the church have compromised. There is an attempt to hold the church hostage by those who will have no tolerance for it; strip away its rights, and remove it from existence. But **Matthew 11:12** states, *"And from the days of John the Baptist until now the kingdom of heaven suffers violence, and the violent take it by force."*

PRAYER

Prayer is a practical way to respond to fear, but one must also realize the best way to pray is to use the Word of God. This means we are counting on faith in God just the same.

"The LORD is my light and my salvation; whom shall I fear? The LORD is the strength of my life; of whom shall I be afraid? When the wicked came against me to eat up my flesh, my enemies and foes, they stumbled and fell. Though an army may encamp against me, my heart shall not fear; though war may rise against me, In this I will be confident." (Psalm 27:1-3).

Praying is applying God's Word to our situation, so we speak what we believe, and we believe what God says. That helps us to do what we say and believe, and we see the results. **2 Corinthians 10:3-5** states, *"For though we walk in the flesh, we do not war according to the flesh. For the weapons of our warfare are not carnal but mighty in God for pulling down strongholds, casting down arguments and every high thing that exalts itself against the knowledge of God, bringing every thought into captivity to the obedience of Christ."*

We can train our thoughts, and we can combat negative thoughts of fears and bring them under the obedience of God's Word. **Philippians 4:6** states, *"Be anxious for nothing, but in everything by prayer and supplication, with thanksgiving, let your requests be made known to God."*

I am used to being in the rural countryside on holidays from school. One summer, I had to walk through a dark area by myself called "Dark Hill." It was so named because even in the daytime, it was dark due to the huge, thick foliage about a quarter of a mile long. That was the only known way home, and I decided God would not let anything happen to me, so I must trust Him.

I sang in a loud voice *"Jesus is the Light of the World"* all the way through Dark Hill. I made it home, and I felt that God had been with me all the way through.

I also believe some people in the church have an unhealthy fear of approaching or praying to God. If you have fear and need help, but are afraid to pray, then fear is blocking you from getting help to get rid of the fear itself.

In the Old Testament, the people of Israel were so afraid of God that they asked Moses to talk to God for them. They even stayed away from the Tent of Meeting. This is found in **Exodus 20**. They actually said, *"Do not let God speak to us or we will die."* I think that even today we would rather have a "priest" pray on our behalf than come *"boldly to the throne of grace"* and find grace to help us in time of need.

> **Psalm 34:1-4** *states, "I will bless the* LORD *at all times; His praise shall continually be in my mouth. My soul shall make its boast in the* LORD*; the humble shall hear of it and be glad. Oh, magnify the* LORD *with me, and let us exalt His name together. I sought the* LORD*, and He heard me, and delivered me from all my fears."*

PEACE

> *"Great peace have those who love Your law, and nothing causes them to stumble."* **(Psalm 119:165).**

Philippians 4 urges us not to be anxious about anything but pray and ask God for help. It goes on to say in verse 7: "... *and the peace of God, which surpasses all understanding, will guard your hearts and minds through Christ Jesus.*"

When your faith in God is intact, and you are confident in God, you will be at peace. Real peace that only comes from God will keep your heart and mind (**Colossians 3:15**).

> *Jesus says: "Peace I leave with you, My peace I give to you; not as the world gives do I give to you. Let not your heart be troubled, neither let it be afraid."* (**St. John 14:27**).

When you are filled with the peace of God, fear no longer has a hold on you.

For some people, prayer and counseling are necessary. You may have one or more of these fears in your life, and maybe by reading this book, you receive enough to be set free. However, if there is no breakthrough or there are some other fears or issues, and no change occurs, please seek biblical counseling from someone who can help. The advantage of counseling is that one can identify the types of fear from talking and observing, then we can pray and apply Scriptures that are fitting to the specific case.

Finding the root cause of one's fear helps manage the fear. Most times it has to do with what we do not yet know; the unknown. If it is fear of the dark, we are uncertain of what lies beyond where we can see. If it is fear of criticism, we are uncertain of what others may say about us. If only we knew, then we probably would not be afraid. Sometimes we have to ask ourselves, What if? What is the worst that can happen? If the worst happens, then what?

Many years ago, I spoke with a young lady who was afraid she was becoming a homosexual. I realized she had never yearned to be or have been involved in such activities, but the thought came to her on several occasions. We then found Scriptures to help her purify her thoughts and *"take every thought captive."* Then we prayed and worshipped. After delving into her childhood for a while, we saw areas where demons of lust could have entered her through no fault of her own. She was eventually set free and is enjoying a meaningful life to this day.

It has been proven that people who pray and/or attend church are less likely to get certain illnesses due to having less stress. Stress increases with fear and anxiety, and we must learn to dump our fears, our cares, and burdens on someone who can help. **1 Peter 5:7** says, *"Casting all your cares upon Him, for He cares for you."* This does not mean we become careless and naïve, but neither do we worry about every little thing, especially things we can do nothing about.

A lot of time and energy is wasted due to fear, and many people have learned, perhaps just out of necessity, to use this energy to solve their dilemma instead. Many women suffering from fear or threats have responded by taking self-defense classes and have turned the tables in their situations. Most times, the lessons go beyond merely providing the confidence to defend themselves but also offer a worthy pastime that boosts their self-esteem after winning awards or gaining acknowledgments.

Elijah had one of his most successful moments as a prophet at Mount Carmel. He was scared to death of Jezebel, who had sent a message that she was going to kill him (**1 Kings 19-20**). Elijah then fled in utter fear. It is ironic that not only did she not kill him, but he never died at all, but was taken up alive by God in a chariot. How many times do we fear things that will never happen?

Other lessons or activities that people have become involved in include swimming, rifle shooting, bodybuilding, and so on. Some people change and feel better just by joining a local club where they no longer feel alone and helpless but make many friends that are constantly in contact and spend much time together. People who are mostly alone are targets, and being part of a church fellowship helps many people in a practical way.

Whatever fears are stopping you from doing what you need to do, you can be delivered. As it states in **Philippians 4:13,** *"I can do all things through Christ who strengthens me."* You can overcome, if you let Him help you. We have had many successful cases, but not all cases end up so well. Not everyone will be honest and open to someone else about their past or their activities and exposure. Many times, we almost set people free, but they refused to continue because of PRIDE.

FEAR OVERVIEW

Here is a summary of this section as well as a few probing questions to get you started on the path to overcoming the restrictions of fear in your life. This summary may prompt you to review the previous chapters, which is good to do. You may want to review some of the more unfamiliar types of fear to determine whether you have experienced any of them. There are many others not mentioned in this book.

IS IT FEAR OR WHAT?

- We were all created for success; wired and pre-packed to win.

- Anything shorting out our success is not necessarily from God.

- Fear is sometimes disguised as something else, such as shyness, patience, and carefulness.

- Fear is used by your enemy to stop you from achieving or performing well.

- Fear can immobilize you, and you don't know why.

- God did not give us the spirit of fear, and fear can become a spirit.

- There are many types of fear.

- One fear may lead to another.

- Fears may have arisen from spoken words or events, movies, or even books that you read.

HAS IT BORNE FRUIT?

- Fear may take root and grow to chronic phobia or paranoia.

- Fear can become a stronghold in one's life and must be broken off with prayer and biblical counsel.

- It may even become so accepted that one no longer believes there can be a change.

- Deep-set fear can lead to suicides for some, and mental illnesses for others.

- Don't let fear stop you.

HARNESSING AND MANAGING FEAR

- You must acknowledge your fears to harness and manage them.

- The energy, time, and effort wasted to run and hide because of fear could be used more productively.

- Most of the things we fear usually never happen to us at all.

- Ask yourself if the worst happened, what would you do to go on?

- Do not be anxious about anything.

- Learn to pray and ask God for help.

- God teaches us to have courage instead of allowing fear to rule us.

- Courage allows us to act, despite the fear.

- Build your faith to better respond to fear.

- Faith gives you peace, the opposite of fear.

- We can use fear to our advantage by channeling the energy into prevention or other activities that will help us be better.

SELF-CHECK REFLECTION

Do you believe you were born for success?

Is there anything preventing you from accomplishing things?

Have you identified any fears in your life?

Think about it, do you excuse it or say it is not too serious?

Can you think of anyone using fear to manipulate you?

Are there things you always wanted to do but don't know why you haven't done them yet?

Is there anything or anyone that you think you are afraid of?

If your answer is yes, why are you afraid of it or them?

Can you identify any fear in someone you know?

What Scripture can you think of that is relevant to each of the fears you identified in someone you know?

How will you apply these Scriptures to your own life?

Do you use fear to manipulate anyone?

Have you ever used courage in the face of fear?

How does using courage in the face of fear make you feel?

Do you think you may need to see someone for counseling?

Will you get some help?

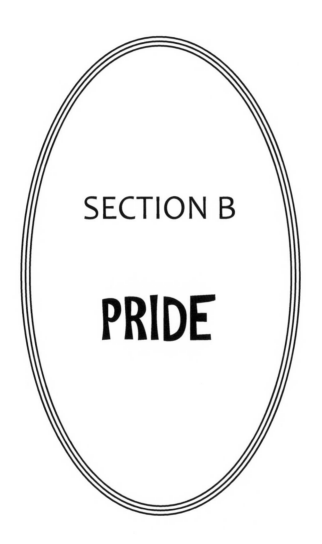

SECTION B

PRIDE

Likewise, you younger people, submit yourselves to *your* elders. Yes, all of *you* be submissive to one another, and be clothed with humility, for "God resists the proud, but gives grace to the humble."

(1 Peter 5:5 – NKJV)

CHAPTER FOUR

LOOK AT ME!

Proverbs 16:18 is one of the most common Bible verses that deal with pride: *"Pride goeth before destruction, and a haughty spirit before a fall."* It warns of the sure and subtle dangers of this root. However, I need to differentiate between positive pride and negative pride. There is productive pride where you take pride in yourself, in what you do, and how you dress and carry yourself. That keeps us on our toes and out of trouble. That helps us be ambitious and not be a loser. Even in church, I tell my audience to have spiritual ambition. There is nothing wrong with wanting to do well and look good. That is what having good self-esteem and being confident is about. However, negative pride says you are better than they are, and they are beneath you.

POSITIVE PRIDE

Let us consider what the Bible says, *"But let each one examine his own work, and then he will have rejoicing in himself alone, and not in another."* **(Galatians 6:4)**.

> **2 Corinthians 10:12-16** *tells us it not wise to compare ourselves with others: "For we dare not class ourselves or compare ourselves with those who commend themselves. But they, measuring themselves by themselves, and comparing themselves among themselves, are not wise. We, however, will not boast beyond measure, but within the limits of the sphere which God appointed us—a sphere which especially includes you. For we are not overextending ourselves (as though our authority did not extend to you), for it was to you that we came with the gospel of Christ; not boasting of things beyond measure, that is, in other men's labors, but having hope, that as your faith is increased, we shall be greatly enlarged by you in our sphere, to preach the gospel in the regions beyond you, and not to boast in another man's sphere of accomplishment."*

The answer lies in Christ and His Word. God gave us a standard to compare to and emulate. Then we can take pride in ourselves alone *and in God.* We can all be 'proud' to exhibit good positive pride. This is healthy self-esteem and is godly, progressive, and even helpful to others. Verse 17 goes on to say, *"But "he who glories, let him glory in the LORD.""* Consider someone who sees you as a role model or a good Christian example. They are not intimidated by you nor do they feel less than or hopelessly lost because they are not exactly like you.

When we get our image identity from God and Jesus Christ, then we can be proud of who we are in Christ. There is a Youth Leadership Training program called **B.O.S.S.**[6] (Building on Spiritual Substance), which teaches the youngsters to respond when asked how they were doing with *"We are perfect in Him!"* I believe positive pride causes us to be admired more than to be envied. There will always be a person who will be envious, but that is their problem. We must be able to separate positive, godly pride from negative pride.

NEGATIVE PRIDE

Negative pride gives a sense of superiority and an air of aboveness that is downright obnoxious. Jesus taught His disciples a valuable lesson, *"Two men went up to the temple to pray, one a Pharisee and the other a tax collector. The Pharisee stood and prayed thus with himself, 'God, I thank You that I am not like other men—extortioners, unjust, adulterers, or even as this tax collector. I fast twice a week; I give tithes of all that I possess.' And the tax collector, standing afar off, would not so much as raise his eyes to heaven, but beat his breast, saying, 'God, be merciful to me a sinner!' I tell you, this man went down to his house justified rather than the other; for everyone who exalts himself will be humbled, and he who humbles himself will be exalted." (Luke 18:10-14)*

Negative pride had the better of the Pharisee, and Jesus pointed that out to His disciples. We do not feel as bad when we compare ourselves to someone we believe is doing worse than we are. When we put others down, we believe we are much better than they are, and we want to feel good about ourselves, so 'hello, negative pride.'

The devil uses pride the way he uses fear, as a deception. He will try to deceive you into thinking that the feeling is good. That is what happened in the Garden of Eden. The devil deceived Eve. He never chose Adam because he knew Adam got his information directly from God. Eve would have been told what God said by her husband. So because Eve had secondhand information, he could try to get her to doubt or second-guess what God really said.

> *He goes around like a roaring lion (fear), and then he says, "'I will ascend into heaven, I will exalt my throne above the stars of God; I will also sit on the mount of the congregation on the farthest sides of the north; I will ascend above the heights of the clouds, I will be like the Most High.' (pride)"* (**Isaiah 14:13b-14**).

Please note that the letter 'I' is in the center of 'pride.' Self-centeredness will always set us up for self-deception.

Ezekiel 28:15 *states that iniquity was found in Satan: "You were perfect in your ways from the day you were* *created, till iniquity was found in you." Notice that he was perfect. Perfectionists are prone to negative pride, if they are not careful.*

*If the devil gets you to agree with his thoughts, then you will make them yours. That is why Paul says we should "bring every thought into captivity to the obedience of Christ" (***2 Corinthians 10:5b).**

This state of mind gives us a sense of false security, which is discussed in **Galatians 6:3***: "For if anyone thinks himself to be something, when he is nothing, he deceives himself."*

C. S. Lewis said it best: *"A proud man is always looking down on things and people; and, of course, as long as you are looking down, you cannot see something that is above you."* [7]

Pride, in the negative form, is a deception; a screen used to prevent us from seeing the true picture and cause us to miss reality. When we are let down by false pride, we become disappointed and frustrated. Many people's lives end in disaster when things do not turn out the way they expected. The people and things in which they placed their confidence proves to be inadequate to support their demands and support, as they were only fleeting and temporal, based on false premises.

The Greek characters Oedipus and Achilles were led to a great downfall by "hubris," that is, excessive pride and over-confidence.

SUBTLETY OF PRIDE

Pride is not always easily discerned by oneself, or others for that matter. Sometimes it is masked, just as fear can be at times. One can also become comfortable with this feeling of pride because, honestly, it feels good. Who does not want to feel, good except when we feel bad that it is causing pain to others? Sadistic behavior is not easily addressed without dealing with underlying issues. So when we become comfortable with this smug feeling, we may not want to change. We will get so used to this feeling that we will not hear or accept any criticism. Therefore, anyone who does not agree with us is against us and is fighting against us, or so we are made to believe.

That is why some people must always have the last say, must have their idea considered, and must be acknowledged or commended. Some people will hold a grudge or become depressed if their names are not called at a particular function. Then there is the title fixation—please don't forget to address them or refer to them using their hard-earned titles. Why should we rob them of the security of fancy titles that put them high on a pedestal? They need it—be kind to them (sarcasm, sorry). Sometimes, protocol dictates that we show respect to those esteemed guests, dignitaries, and leaders, as also required in Scriptures.

Submit to governing authorities and respect those in authority, for all authority is from God: *"Let every soul be subject to the governing authorities. For there is no authority except from God, and the authorities that exist are appointed by God."* **(Romans 13:1).**

> *In* **1 Peter 2:13-14,** *it states: "Therefore submit yourselves to every ordinance of man for the Lord's sake, whether to the king as supreme, or to governors, as to those who are sent by him for the punishment of evildoers and for the praise of those who do good."*

I have seen people get sick at crucial times in their lives because they are not getting their regular doses of "attention." A colleague in a Christian organization had this problem that we had to deal with continually. It started affecting ministry as well as young Christians who never understood what was happening. A lot of time and effort was spent doing "deliverance ministry" that was not necessary because it was not going to help. His problem was negative pride that held him hostage and hindered his ministry.

Now we must understand that not every problem will be solved by casting out a demon. Sometimes we need to read the Word of God and believe it and agree with God so we can obey Him. The devils will not move from where they have permission to be, without one who has authority revoking that privilege. This is usually done by the one who gave that privilege in the first place or someone higher up in authority.

A dangerous place for negative pride is inside the church. Remember, Lucifer was in heaven when he was overtaken with pride and decided to try to upstage God. He was beautifully adorned, and he was an archangel. He was a specimen of an angel. He led worship and made music directly from his body. He was it! Or so he thought. That is why he tries to deceive us by promising us things in exchange for loyalty. He tried it when he tempted Jesus in the wilderness. He has made pacts with many people and he 'anoints' them in the arts with music, extraordinary skills and fame. Have you ever wondered why the early church was against using traditional music? In the New Testament, a lot of the music was tainted with pagan worship, as we may see in our own history; the early church leaders did not want the confusion.

Musical instruments started to find its way back into the early church in about the seventh century A.D. [8]

So, how does pride affect us, apart from making one seem obnoxious or otherwise bossy, and a "show off"? Well, as with fear, we can miss great opportunities because people avoid us, even if we do not know it.

I can think of a few people who have been severely affected by being filled with pride.

Miss Queen seldom smiles, except when she is being praised or admired or is having a pleasant conversation with someone she likes. She is most often found complaining about others or bragging about what she does to help people. What this 'Christian' lady is not aware of, however, is that few people care to be in her presence because of her distasteful behavior, and those who do, feel they just have to put up with her for now. She seems to look on others with disdain and then complain about a lack of cooperation from people.

If you often have to force people to do what you want them to do, then check how people feel about you. You may be making yourself into something that you are not to please people who don't appreciate you for who you are. Many people who 'hype' with you are just there for the good times; they use you, but they don't care deeply about you.

The sin of negative pride is comparison, as you saw earlier. If you are constantly trying to measure up, then you might be measuring down to the wrong standard. You will feel like a failure if you don't have someone to compare with to feel 'better than.'

Not only will you lose out in relationships, but you will also oppress and depress people knowingly or unknowingly. Do not make yourself available to the enemy to be used to abuse people.

CHAPTER FIVE

HUMILITY

We cannot speak about pride without mentioning humility. Humility is the opposite of pride and must be examined if one is to understand how to deal with pride effectively. There is, however, false or negative humility, something that is common but not spoken about much.

FALSE HUMILITY

Many people do not accept certain offers or positions because they believe it would put them in the limelight too much and that would make them proud. These people underperform or even miss their calling in life because they have been taught to remain humble. When we consider stepping up our performance, we compare ourselves to others already performing at that level. It is not whether it is the right thing to do but can I really do that, instead of can God do that?

If I keep comparing my weaknesses to your strengths, I may soon end up with a negative self-image. Self-deprecation is a grueling, harmful poison to the spirit and mind. As harmful as it is to think more highly of yourself than you ought, thinking too lowly of yourself will sentence you to a life of mediocrity.[9]

Many people are filled with potential and great ability but will not move forward because they have been told it is not their place. They must bear the cross they have been given. They are not like this person or that other person, and what they are thinking about is just not for them. This wrong thinking is just as dangerous as fear. It prevents people from fulfilling their purpose in God and from being a significant contributor to society.

Just as the sin of pride is one of comparison, so is the deception of false humility. We can compare ourselves to someone else and choose not to proceed with an action that is right by saying, 'I will be humble' or 'I will humble myself.' This is a major mistake made by many people, especially in church. It is never wrong to aspire to do good or allow God to use us as best as He sees fit, even if that means going up on a stage, being in broadcast media, or anything that puts you directly in the public's eye.

There is also FAKE HUMILITY, where someone pretends to be humble intending to deceive.

Consider Ahaz in **Isaiah 7:10-12**. He refused God's instruction, citing humility as the reason: *Moreover the L*ORD *spoke again to Ahaz, saying, "Ask a sign for yourself from the L*ORD *your God; ask it either in the depth or in the height above." But Ahaz said, "I will not ask, nor will I test the L*ORD*!"*

That was a blatant disobedient act by Ahaz, and his excuse was also classical. The phrase, *"I will not put the Lord to the test,"* was meant to deceive and was not one of humility and respect for God. There are times when God asks us to test and prove Him, and this was one such moment. As **Malachi 3:10** states: *"Bring all the tithes into the storehouse, that there may be food in My house, and try Me now in this," says the L*ORD *of hosts, "If I will not open for you the windows of heaven and pour out for you such blessing that there will not be room enough to receive it."*

Then there is the example of King Saul in **1 Samuel 13:11-12**. Because of fear of his enemies and presumption, he offered the sacrifice that should have been made by the prophet, " And Samuel said, "What have you done?" Saul said, "When I saw that the people were scattered from me, and *that* you did not come within the days appointed, and *that* the Philistines gathered together at Michmash, then I said, 'The Philistines will now come down on me at Gilgal, and I have not made supplication to the L*ORD*.' Therefore I felt compelled, and offered a burnt offering.""

Here the king made that grand excuse, *"I have not made supplication to the LORD."* Other translations state, *"I have not sought the Lord."* This is a religious excuse, one that has been sanitized here by fake humility, trying to justify disobedience to let it look right under the circumstances. 'Seeking the Lord' can sound spiritual but can also be a timely excuse when we don't want to do something, hence, *'I have to pray about it.'*

Paul warns about this in **Colossians 2:18-19**, describing these acts of deception. There were people boasting and delighting in being seen as humble. Some even impose on others certain actions that are not done from a repentant heart but leads to false worship:

"Let no one cheat you of your reward, taking delight in false humility and worship of angels, intruding into those things which he has not seen, vainly puffed up by his fleshly mind, and not holding fast to the Head, from whom all the body, nourished and knit together by joints and ligaments, grows with the increase that is from God. Therefore, if you died with Christ from the basic principles of the world, why, as though living in the world, do you subject yourselves to regulations— "Do not touch, do not taste, do not handle," which all concern things which perish with the using—according to the commandments and doctrines of men? These things indeed have an appearance of wisdom in self-imposed religion, false humility, and neglect of the body, but are of no value against the indulgence of the flesh."

It seems one filled with pride is also prone to false humility.

TRUE HUMILITY

Humility has more to do with faith than it has to do with pride. My personal definition of humility is **"true dependence on God."** If one is truly dependent on God, it is impossible to be filled with pride. The nature of the worship of God is intrinsically inclined to dependence and submission to God. One can be humble and confident, having good healthy pride in what they do and in who they are without looking down on others.

> *Consider the Scripture in* **Romans 12:3.** *Here the Apostle Paul writes: "For I say, through the grace given to me, to everyone who is among you, not to think of himself more highly than he ought to think, but to think soberly, as God has dealt to each one a measure of faith."*

He goes on to talk about the body and the members needing each other. We should not be in competition with each other, but each person should work according to his faith, according to his dependence on God to help to do what God has called him to. We all have been given the measure of faith, and we all have been given gifts, talents, and abilities. We all have something to work with, and we are called to do only what we can do and to do it the way God wants it done.

Every person has to give an account to God alone for the life we live. We will not be able to say, I did not do what I should have done because I am not like John or Jim.

We will be more disappointed when we realize that we wasted so much time trying to impress people, trying to be like others, and trying to compete with some.

Pleasing God is more important than pleasing people, and we should not please people at the expense of pleasing God. While God wants us to love our neighbors and be good to others, we must not lose sight of the fact that He works in us to accomplish this. All glory ultimately comes from Him (God) and goes to Him through us. Also, we work with Him to bring others to Him and glorify Him. Now that gives Him glory!

If we must compare, then compare ourselves with the Word of God, with Christ as our example. No competition is needed between the sons of God. This may not be so practical if you are not a Christian, but you can learn from it.

When we compare ourselves to those weaker than we are, we can become egotistically proud, and when we compare ourselves with those stronger than we are, we can put ourselves down too much. Try Jesus!

THE CURE FOR COMPARISON

Accept yourself as God has made you. You are who God made you to be; you are unique. Different is what makes you significant and gives you the edge without making you obnoxious or oppressive to others. What God has given you may be so different from what others have that if you focus on what others have, it may throw you off course. Accept who you are and what you have.

A lot of our problems are solved once we accept ourselves and find out what God has given us to do and what He wants us to do. Then we can proceed to do the job at hand, and that is the priority. Don't waste a lot of time trying to do what others are doing, and trying to be what others are called to be.

Seek to please God and do what He wants. When we are at peace about what we are here for, we live a peaceful life without strife and give more meaning to humanity. We then please God, instead of being preoccupied with non-essentials doing, *"all to the glory of God"* (**1 Corinthians 10:31b**).

> *"And whatever you do in word or deed, do all in the name of the Lord Jesus, giving thanks to God the Father through Him."* (**Colossians 3:17**).

Dr. Morris Sheats puts it this way, *"As long as you compare yourself with others, the chances are that you will not be emotionally whole. God has asked you to be happy with the person you are; to accept yourself. When you do that, you are free from the sin of comparison."* [10]

Finally, humility has more to do with how we relate to others than how we look, what we have, and what we have done. Jesus taught His disciples not to laud it over the people, but to serve them: *And He sat down, called the twelve, and said to them, "If anyone desires to be first, he shall be last of all and servant of all."* (**Mark 9:35**).

> *In* **Mark 10:44** *it says, "And whoever of you desires to be first shall be slave of all."*

CHAPTER SIX

RIGHT RESPONSE

Maybe you think you don't have a problem with pride. Great, but before we finish this section, let us look at some questions.

Do you like to be heard? We all have a voice and an opinion, and when we are heard, it feels good. We all like the sound of our own voices but some of us more than others. Must you have the last word? Ask your friends and family members, because it may not feel that way to you.

Do you like to be seen? Sure, we all should think we have a place, a niche in the scheme of things. When we are spoken about favorably, that feels good. We all like a compliment; that is normal. Some of us have to be seen by everybody and be validated, or we just don't feel right.

Do you find it easy to say you are sorry? Even if you are right, do you insist on your rights and winning the argument?

How about criticisms? Can you handle constructive criticism, or do you have to argue it out first? Do you pout? How about criticisms that are just downright unfair? Can you handle it without creating a scene?

CONFIDENCE

By accepting ourselves and the gifts and calling God has given us, we will live our lives in confidence. God-confidence is superior to self-confidence, which makes us self-dependent instead of God dependent. This means that, *"I know who I am"* and am confident in what I do. We also have faith and trust in God to enable us to do what He wants done. He says in **James 4:6** that, *"God resists the proud, but gives grace to the humble."* When we humble ourselves and depend on God, He enables us. *'Giving grace'* means enabling.

> *In* **Matthew 6:27**, *Jesus asks, "Which of you by worrying can add one cubit to his stature?"*

Jesus gave a lengthy discourse on religious pride in **Matthew 23**. Here He describes how the teachers of the law and the Pharisees burdened the people and were unwilling to help them with their burdens. A humble person seeks to help, instead of hinder. They add to the quality of life of others, not subtract from it.

> *Let us look at* **verses 5 to 7**, *"But all their works they do to be seen by men. They make their phylacteries broad and enlarge the borders of their garments. They love the best places at feasts, the best seats in the synagogues, greetings in the marketplaces, and to be called by men, 'Rabbi, Rabbi.'"*

> *As Jesus continues to teach us humility, He says, "But he who is greatest among you shall be your servant. And whoever exalts himself will be humbled, and he who humbles himself will be exalted."* **(Matthew 23:11-12)**

He then goes on to show their priorities were all wrong. Maybe we should reexamine our priorities by His standard.

LOVE

Love should be the motive for our actions, as God's creation. We are creatures created in His likeness, and He is love. We all want love and enjoy the good feeling we get when we love someone else. So to love, we have to give, and that means serving someone else's need.

Those who struggle the most with pride are those in a position to lead others. In **Matthew 6,** Jesus speaks about doing things for others to see us, which will not bring lasting reward. What we do primarily to please God will be rewarded by Him openly and lastingly.

In the church, we call it ministry, and those of us who are ministers are just simply 'servants.' Do we serve in humility with love to please God or do we become pompous and hearty, 'lording' it over those we serve?

Love covers a multitude of sins, and if you really love your neighbor, you ought to tell them, *"You are filled with bad pride; it is not good for you."*

We should not embarrass them, but be kind enough to tell them they are headed for a fall.

Many people have been overcome with pride because others have heaped on them an unhealthy amount of praise and adulation to the point of human worship. This happens with politicians, pop stars, and some pastors. We must realize that when we do this, we are in fact lying and giving the devil, the father of lies, a reason to fertilize these lies. This makes them even bigger, and then they explode into a cult or a dictatorship. Consider the exaggerated praises we heap on our pastors before they preach on Sunday morning. When this happens, we must fight to remind ourselves that we are here to worship and praise God, not a man.

How about when we pray and when we are in a corporate worship setting?

I remember hearing the question in my head once, *"If you opened your eyes right now and the seats were empty, no one else there, would your prayer continue the way it is going right now?"* I had to think about that, and I soon decided no one else will affect my prayer or my worship to God.

Another time, the same thing happened with my dress code. Was I really dressing to please God or was I dressing to please those people who will turn up at church? Will my prayer, worship, or dress impress God or the people? Can this even impress God?

Do I owe it to you to let you know that your ego is just a little too high? Does love dictate that I graciously and humbly tell you the truth?

We tend not to address pride in someone else because of fear, and we tend not to address pride in our own lives out of ignorance. Ignorance will be covered in our next section.

WORSHIP

True humility is dependence on God. When we acknowledge God for who He is, we *"humble ourselves in the mighty hand of God,"* knowing that we have nothing except what He has given us. We can do nothing except what He has enabled us to do and has allowed. Seeing His greatness, power, and authority, we submit to Him and worship Him.

One who truly worships God, that is, worship Him in Spirit and truth, is truly humble. This means we have found our identity in the One who made us, and we are good with that. We become confident in Him, confident in ourselves, and we are safe in Him. Our lives are *"hidden with Christ in God"* **(Colossians 3:3b)**. We are who we are, and we know who we are.

PRIDE OVERVIEW

Here are a few reminders from this section:

- Pride is the most dangerous and subtle of these three roots.

- There is positive pride and negative pride.

- Both negative pride and false humility are sins of comparison.

- Negative pride results in thinking too highly of oneself.

- False humility results in low self-worth and poor performance.

- True humility results in a healthy self-esteem and godly identity.

- True humility is depending on God, who is greater than we are.
- True humility is accepting you as perfect in Him. God loves you!
- Finding your identity in God, through Jesus His Son, gives one true humility and positive pride.
- Jesus and God's Word should be our standard.
- We should not exalt humans, and make them like God.
- Negative pride will cause abuse to or neglect of others.
- Worship only God.

SELF-CHECK REFLECTION

Do you often compare yourself to people who are 'better,' do better, and have more than yourself?

How do you feel about yourself when you compare with them?

Do you compare yourself with people who are 'lesser,' do less, and have less than yourself?

How do you feel about yourself when you compare with them?

Do you think of yourself more highly than you ought? *(Romans 12:3)*

Ask someone whom you trust to tell you what they think about your pride level and take note.

If you believe you need help with negative pride or false humility, seek biblical counsel. Will you?

Can you think of a reason why you would NOT seek Biblical Counsel?

If you are not a born-again believer in Jesus Christ, you may need to accept Him as your personal Lord and Savior to get the most out of this.

Decide that you want to, then tell Him in prayer. See ***Romans 10:9-10.***

Learn to worship truly.

SECTION C

IGNORANCE

My people are destroyed for lack of knowledge.

(Hosea 4:6a – NKJV)

CHAPTER SEVEN

HE WHO KNOWS

Hosea 4:6 says, *"My people are destroyed for lack of knowledge."* This is a readily quoted Bible text; however, this does not apply only to spiritual things, as 'perish' here means **being destroyed**. 'Lack of knowledge' here really means **rejecting knowledge**.

Anyone who despises knowledge is headed for failure, destruction, and frustration in life. Knowledge is the key to success in anything one undertakes. I find it interesting that the things many people believe are extremely difficult or impossible, somebody else is already doing.

Therefore, it only seems next to impossible when you don't know how. Anything is difficult to do when you don't know how to do it. Once you know how to do it, then it becomes easy.

THE WISE

The old Arabic proverb states that, *"He who knows and knows he knows is wise, seek him."*

Knowledge without wisdom and understanding still leave us coming up short. The Bible teaches us to seek wisdom, but get understanding also **(Proverbs 4:5-9).** Many people are extremely knowledgeable, but lack wisdom and understanding of the issues and situation they are in. Knowledge puffs up. Paul says, *"Now concerning things offered to idols: We know that we all have knowledge. Knowledge puffs up, but love edifies. And if anyone thinks that he knows anything, he knows nothing yet as he ought to know. But if anyone loves God, this one is known by Him."* **(1 Corinthians 8:1-3).**

Therefore, if one has knowledge with neither wisdom nor understanding in the matter, one needs help.

Failure is almost guaranteed if you have knowledge but don't know how to apply such knowledge in a particular situation. If you are not humble enough to ask for help because you are puffed up with pride or choose to order people around to cover up your shortcomings due to fear; you need help!

Most of the book of Proverbs teaches us to seek wisdom, but it also teaches us to seek counsel. How often do we seek the expert in an area for advice on an issue, whether it be cars or computers, psychology or theology? Many grave mistakes have been made by people who never knew what they were doing.

> *"A wise man is strong, yes, a man of knowledge increases strength; for by wise counsel you will wage your own war, and in a multitude of counselors there is safety." (**Proverbs 24:5-6**).*

ASLEEP IN ZION

An old proverb says: *"He who knows and knows not he knows, is asleep, wake him."*

Have you ever seen people who know a lot but are never putting what they know into practice? Yes, I have too. Many people are not fulfilling anything great because they are not using what they have. Most times they are seeking something else that they don't have and are not gifted or called for.

Nowhere is this more telling than in the body of Christ. The Church of Jesus Christ has the Word of God, the Living Word, and The Holy Spirit of God, who uses this Word as a sword. How can a body of people have so much knowledge available to them and make so many mistakes? Most times, the knowledge is there, but we forget it. We fall asleep on the job sometimes; we are too comfortable. Coach Al Hollingsworth encourages his students to *"stay conscious and do not go unconscious in life."* He states, *"Unconscious people who wait are no threat to Satan and no help to God."* [11]

A sleeping or unconscious person is like a dead man; he is of no use to anyone while he is down and out. It can be so sad if we are alive, full of potential, knowledge, and wisdom but of no use to anyone.

So *"Awake, Zion, awake; awake and trim your lamps!"* Individuals make up the church, and we are enamored with large gatherings, but each one of us needs to respond. Each man or women of God need to arise and be counted and respond to the world around us in a godly way. We must stay conscious and wake our brethren. This is war!

Paul declares in **1 Corinthians 2:16b**, *"We have the mind of Christ."* Therefore, even if we don't know about the issue, God knows, and we have access to it through Jesus Christ. This is not a popular concept, since it borders on being 'kooky.' But consider the Scriptures as well as past experiences to see if you really know God. It is not hype or fantasy; God reveals many things to us at times. Have you ever had a dream that turns out exactly the way you saw it?

How about in worship? Have you ever had a vision in the middle of worship, or hear an audible voice or just whatever way God chose to reveal something to you? Have you ever had the experience of seeing a gift or a manifestation of discernment, Word of Knowledge, or Word of Wisdom on display? (**1 Corinthians 12:8**).

CHAPTER EIGHT

HE WHO KNOWS NOT

A lot can be said about the vast amount of knowledge in the world. More astounding is the large number of people who think they know so much. People walk around every day looking smug because they have studied extensively in a particular field. Well, when you know, you know; and when you don't know, well...

A CHILD IS TEACHABLE

An old proverb says, *"He who knows not and knows he knows not, he is a child, teach him."*

*What I like about this sentiment is that children are mostly trusting and teachable. Jesus says, "Assuredly, I say to you, unless you are converted and become as little children, you will by no means enter the kingdom of heaven. Therefore whoever humbles himself as this little child is the greatest in the kingdom of heaven. Whoever receives one little child like this in My name receives Me." (***Matthew 18:3-5***).*

Jesus also says, "Take My yoke upon you and learn from Me, for I am gentle and lowly in heart, and you will find rest for your souls. For My yoke is easy and My burden is light." (**Matthew 11:29-30**).

Not knowing is not an excuse. We have the Word of God available; we hear it being preached all the time and everywhere. Also, **Romans 1:20** states: *"For since the creation of the world His invisible attributes are clearly seen, being understood by the things that are made, even His eternal power and Godhead, so that they are without excuse."*

We can learn the truth about God through His Word. The Scriptures invite us to learn, to get to know, that is, get knowledge of Him so we can put our faith in Him. As we saw in the previous chapter, we are encouraged to seek knowledge, wisdom, and understanding. We have to go get it and ask for it, and that takes a little humility. Research has shown that there are over five thousand promises in the Bible that God has given us. If we don't know them, we cannot accept them, or request and claim them when we don't see them.

Would you ask a carpenter to help you fix your computer or a tailor to repair your roof? Then why do we take chances with our lives instead of asking the One who gave us life to help us understand it and make sense of it?

A FOOL'S HEART

An old proverb says, *"He who knows not and knows not he knows not is a fool, shun him!"*

How wise can you be if you think you know something and then find out you were mistaken?

"The fool has said in his heart, 'there is no God'" (**Psalm 14:1**), yet many of us live as if there is no God and life doesn't matter, black or white. Are we not, therefore, behaving as the fool if we have no knowledge of God? The author of life has given us the manual for life, yet we despise it and choose to make God into our own image instead of worshiping Him alone as God.

A few years ago, a friend said, *"It is amazing how much we have to know to learn and realize that we really don't know much."*

> **Isaiah 5:13** *says, "Therefore my people have gone into captivity, because they have no knowledge; their honorable men are famished, and their multitude dried up with thirst."*

Without the right information and the wisdom and understanding to use it, we will not be able to do what needs to be done for success in life.

Consider **Romans 1:21:** *"because, although they knew God, they did not glorify Him as God, nor were thankful, but became futile in their thoughts, and their foolish hearts were darkened."*

Man *'knew of God.'* He *'knew about'* but did not seek to truly *'know,'* that is, intimately to worship and adore Him for who He is.

IN THE DARK

In the Scripture, darkness is sometimes used to refer to ignorance while light is used to refer to knowledge. Many Christians are kept in the dark in the area of witchcraft and the occult. They either refuse to admit that such things exist or they are overly obsessed with meaningless outbursts that are of no effect. The Bible is filled with many passages that can teach us about the occult and these practices, and we can get knowledgeable in this area. Spiritual strongholds, curses, and just plain lack of knowledge prevent us from advancing in so many areas of our lives, but we just don't know.

DECEPTION

C. S. Lewis wrote in his *Screwtape Letters*: *"There are two equal and opposite errors into which our race can fall about the devil, one is disbelief in their existence. The other is to believe, and to feel an excessive and unhealthy interest in them. They themselves are equally pleased with both errors."* [12]

James said in **James 1:5,** *"If any of you lacks wisdom, let him ask of God, who gives to all liberally and without reproach, and it will be given to him."*

Sometimes we go astray and have 'forgotten' that God has better things for us. This convenient loss of memory is ignorance. **Hebrews 5:2 states,** *"He can have compassion on those who are ignorant and going astray, since he himself is also subject to weakness."* This refers to the earthly high priest, who himself is prone to 'forgetting' as well.

The story of the prodigal son also tells how we can be ignorant, though we have been taught and reminded of the right way all along. When the young son squandered all he had, the Bible says, *"But when he came to himself, he said, 'How many of my father's hired servants have bread enough and to spare, and I perish with hunger! I will arise and go to my father, and will say to him, "Father, I have sinned against heaven and before you."'"* **(Luke 15:17-18).**

Ignorance is most times ignoring what God has already set forth and established for our good. **Romans 1:19-21** states that, *"because what may be known of God is manifest in them, for God has shown it to them. For since the creation of the world His invisible attributes are clearly seen, being understood by the things that are made, even His eternal power and Godhead, so that they are without excuse, because, although they knew God, they did not glorify Him as God, nor were thankful, but became futile in their thoughts, and their foolish hearts were darkened."*

We defy Him at our own peril. The God of this age has 'blinded' their eyes.

Consider what Gary Collins said, *"For example, the biblically unsupported ideas that we are saved by good works, that Christians growth depends entirely on ourselves, that doubt or our sexual urges will arouse God's wrath, that God's love depends on our personal actions."* [13]

CHAPTER NINE

HE WHO KNOWS GOD

The man or woman who truly knows God, not just knowing that God exists, but who has an intimate knowledge of God, has a lot going in their favor.

J. I. Packer in his book, *Knowing God*, states that: *"Those who know God:*

1) Have great energy for God
2) Have great boldness for God
3) Have great contentment with God" [14]

The Bible says, "but the people who know their God shall be strong, and carry out exploits" **(Daniel 11:32b)**. *Jesus puts it like this: "And you shall know the truth, and the truth shall make you free"* **(John 8:32)**, *and, again: "Therefore if the Son makes you free, you shall be free indeed"* **(John 8:36).**

It is God who says, "For it is the God who commanded light to shine out of darkness, who has shone in our hearts to give the light of the knowledge of the glory of God in the face of Jesus Christ" **(2 Corinthians 4:6).**

It is in the face of Christ that we find the glory. Let His light shine on you so that you can know Him. He who knows God, knows Christ. In his book, *Purpose Driven Life*, Rick Warren says it this way, *"It is only in God that we discover our origin, our identity, our meaning, our purpose, our significance, and our destiny."*[15]

Maybe the way to conquer one's fear is to humble one's self and submit to God. Maybe the way to overcome one's pride is to get to know God intimately and perhaps the way to really know God is to trust Him, not be afraid of Him, but fear Him in awe and reverence.

This leads to us being totally dependent on Him. **1 Peter 5:5-7** states, *"Likewise you younger people, submit yourselves to your elders. Yes, all of you be submissive to one another, and be clothed with humility, for "God resists the proud,* *but gives grace to the humble." Therefore humble yourselves under the mighty hand of God, that He may exalt you in due time, casting all your care upon Him, for He cares for you."*

You can trust God with your fears and give him all your pride and prejudices. You can seek Him for wisdom in all areas of life. Many people have learned to read after becoming a Christian; many others have gained knowledge in various areas after turning to God. Consider the following true story:

A young man named Louie had been illiterate through no fault of his own and was unable to get a decent job. I remember when he came to our house and started going to church. He eventually became a committed Christian and set out to learn to read the Bible on his own. He frequently asked the pronunciation of words but also their meanings. In a relatively short time, Louie had learned to read and also got a job. Today, he is married and still serving God with his whole heart.

DREAMS AND VISIONS

In the Bible, God reveals information to His servants, and supernatural revelation still happens today.

Daniel and the three Hebrew boys were endowed with ten times more wisdom than their peers. **Daniel 1:19-20** reads, *"Then the king interviewed them, and among them all none was found like Daniel, Hananiah, Mishael, and Azariah; therefore they served before the king. And in all matters of wisdom and understanding about which the king examined them, he found them ten times better than all the magicians and astrologers who were in all his realm."*

> *Joseph was given the interpretation of dreams by God: "When the chief baker saw that the interpretation was good, he said to Joseph, "I also was in my dream, and there were three white baskets on my head.""* **(Genesis 40:16)**.

The Apostle Paul and John were given clear visions from God about things that would take place.

A member of our church shared a dream some time ago and now sees its fulfillment being played out right before her eyes.

God is indeed all-wise and all-knowing, and knowing Him personally is indeed life transforming.

Here is what John Stott says, *"There is evidence for the deity of Jesus – good, strong, historical, cumulative evidence; evidence to which an honest person can subscribe without committing intellectual suicide. But we have to translate our beliefs into deeds. We must humble ourselves before Him. We must trust in him as our Savior and submit to him as our Lord; and then go on to take our place as loyal members of the church and responsible citizens in our community."* [16]

IGNORANCE OVERVIEW

Getting knowledge is important.

- Getting wisdom is even better, as this is the skill to use knowledge.

- Getting understanding is vital to the use of knowledge, as this also involves discernment.

- One should seek counsel and advice where possible.

- Knowledge, by itself, puffs up and feeds into pride.

- It is a fool who says in his heart there is no knowledge.

- Denying the wisdom and knowledge of God is ultimate ignorance.

- Ignoring the laws and instruction of God is ignorance and leads to destruction.

- Fear (reverence and respect) of God is the beginning of wisdom.

- Knowing God brings confidence and favor in one's life.

SELF-CHECK REFLECTION

How knowledgeable are you in the area of your career choice?

Do you have a good understanding of how to apply the knowledge you have?

When you need added information, do you ask for it?

Do you believe in godly wisdom?

Do you ask God for guidance?

CHAPTER TEN

THE FINAL CHAPTER

Many people have conquered their fears, overcame pride, and are increasing in the knowledge of life and God. These success stories are great motivation for us to also master our fears and not let them master us; to turn pride around and be a positive force in life, becoming more knowledgeable, wiser, and to better understand the world in which we live.

Positive seeds and positive roots from the Word of God help us fulfill our purpose. There is also the *Tree of Life* from which to feed, also called the True Vine, and tended by the Father Himself, the Husbandman. This Tree is Jesus! The one we want to be like, *"the Tree planted by the River of life, whose leaves never withers and does not fear when heat comes."* Excerpts taken from **Jeremiah 17:8, Psalm 1:3, and St. John 15.**

A WOMAN OF FAITH

Sue Chen was a seemingly fragile, quiet, and shy young girl studying on the University Campus. Anyone of noble character who saw Sue wanted to look out for her and protect her. She was prone to be hit on by the guys and would certainly be taken advantage of by the "wolves."

There was, however, one thing about Sue. She had given her life to the Lord and was ferociously learning the Word of God. She learned to worship and, most of all, she learned to pray and intercede for others. By practicing the truth of the Scriptures and caring about other people enough to pray for them, Sue soon learned what we called warfare prayer.

This transformed her life immensely, and Sue, though still quiet and unassuming, was never afraid of the largest and loudest of people—neither the devil nor evil spirits—she would take them on in an instant and prevail. I will always remember Sue for her boldness in God. She is a consummate example of someone who has conquered fear and has a sound grasp of Scriptures demonstrably applied to her life. *"I CAN do all things through Christ who strengthens me,"* she would say with conviction and confidence that is surely a real testimony. She was, of course, quoting **Philippians 4:13.**

A MAN WHOSE CONFIDENCE IS IN GOD

My friend Hugh Langley was an angry teenager at school, prone to violence and getting into all sorts of trouble with teachers. Not to mention his failing grades. One afternoon, he was invited to the Christian Fellowship group meeting by a friend and decided to see what it was all about. He ended up becoming a Christian and remarkably stopped getting angry at people and getting into trouble with teachers. His grades went *'through the roof,'* and he became an honor student.

The most astounding change in Hugh was that he went from a proud, selfish, and arrogant boy to the most humble, polite, and caring human being I have ever met. His humility was real, and he had positive pride. Becoming a Christian never made him a 'push-over' by any stretch of the imagination; he was well able to relate to all kinds of people confidently. This was well demonstrated in his ability to reason with the unsavory characters in their element of comfort, but also with professors and judges alike.

He knew who he was and **WHO GOD SAID HE WAS.** He was confident in who God made him to be. He loved the Bible, and we studied it together. For example, **Philippians 1:6** says, *"being confident of this very thing, that He who has begun a good work in you will complete it until the day of Jesus Christ."*

I can hear him say, *"I know who I AM!"*

THE MAN WHO KNOWS GOD

Many people consider themselves knowledgeable, and others consider themselves intelligent and well educated. It is indeed sobering to realize that we do not know as much as we ought to.

Marlon Banfield admitted to wasting time in school, to the ire of his father, and was disappointed in how his life was turning out. He, however, was never a rude or boisterous youngster but had lots of friends and he loved sports. He spent a lot of time playing sports to the detriment of other things that were more important at the time.

It seems that somewhere along the way, Marlon attended church and, seeking to change his life, and he agreed to become a Christian. This changed his life gradually, and he eventually got baptized. He made a surprising turnaround after signing up for a new course in something he liked doing well. He was top of his class and graduated with honors. He testified that he could not have done it without God's help and that by praying and trusting God, he remembered all he needed to know for his exams.

Marlon is now an active Christian, and knowing God has given him enough knowledge to navigate life in these trying times. According to **1 John 5:13**, *"These things I have written to you who believe in the name of the Son of God, that you may know that you have eternal life, and that you may continue to believe in the name* *of the Son of God."* This young man knows that God is with him, for him, and in him and that is the most important thing for him. Once I heard him say, **"I KNOW,** *nobody has to tell me."* Knowing God as your Savior, Father, and Friend surpasses all knowledge.

THE LEADER

One who benefits the most from these writings is the church leader, with the challenges of finding solutions for the parishioner who has blocks and hindrances in their lives. There seems to be something preventing them from moving forward. Many times, these men and women have ambitions of achieving great things, but are never able to move beyond a certain point. Root causes are not always easily identified; in fact, most times, what we think they are as leaders often turn out to be something else. Consider the three basic roots that we have dealt with in this book, and their far-reaching effects and symptoms can help us identify them in people's lives.

Self-checking can go a long way in helping, as it is sometimes better to admit to ourselves than to others the ugly underside of our personalities. Some people, however, have to be confronted head-on or, as a colleague once put it, the 'carefrontation' approach. May God help us as we give ourselves to Him to be used to help as many as we can, unearth the "three" roots and overcome them.

If you are not complete in Him, you too can be made whole; you can be emotionally whole. Jesus came to make us whole again, to restore to us what the enemy of our souls has stolen from us.

We invite you to make Jesus Lord of your life, and you will never be the same again. When He is your Lord, you can always depend on Him to help you in times of trouble.

YOUR WORST FEARS

After speaking with many people, I have found that these three roots affect us in some of the most unexpected ways. Couples and even married couples go for exorbitantly long periods without having sexual intercourse. One of the reasons I have found is due to fear of rejection coming from past experiences or even with each other.

People who love each other are extremely vulnerable to each other and, therefore, emotionally exposed to be hurt at any time by the ones they love most. The man would rather avoid the drama of approaching her for sex. Instead, he seeks a commercial client where service comes as you like it, when you like it, and with excellent customer service. This is never ideal or right by any means, but these 'manly' men, most times, are afraid of the response from the one who should be most accommodating.

They are defrauded, even as Christian men and women. Many women in marriages are afraid of being turned down by a seemingly busy husband, because the last time was so humiliating in her mind. Now she lies in bed fantasizing about somebody else.

Seek help. Don't let fear prevent you from getting help from a professional counselor or a church leader that both of you trust.

Whatever your worst fears are, the thing you fear the most, there is an answer to your dilemma. Good communication in a marital relationship can so easily save our marriages, if we know how.

> **Hebrews 2:14-15** *states, "Inasmuch then as the children have partaken of flesh and blood, He Himself likewise shared in the same, that through death He might destroy him who had the power of death, that is, the devil, and release those who through fear of death were all their lifetime subject to bondage."*

You can be delivered and rescued from your fears. The thing you fear may never happen. Then again, what if it does? If you are prepared to face the consequences, you are no more in bondage to that fear.

Be prepared for eternity, and you never have to fear anything in life.

SELF-ENGROSSED PRIDE

> *Let the lowly brother glory in his exaltation, but the rich in his humiliation, because as a flower of the field he will pass away. For no sooner has the sun risen with a burning heat than it withers the grass; its flower falls, and its beautiful appearance perishes. So the rich man also will fade away in his pursuits.* **(James 1:9-11)**

Let us not put our confidence in things or the *'arm of flesh'* that will fail, for only what is truly done for Christ will last.

THE LIGHT OF HIS KNOWLEDGE

*This is the message which we have heard from Him and declare to you, that God is light and in Him is no darkness at all. If we say that we have fellowship with Him, and walk in darkness, we lie and do not practice the truth. But if we walk in the light as He is in the light, we have fellowship with one another, and the blood of Jesus Christ His Son cleanses us from all sin. (***1 John 1:5-7***).*

Knowledge of God is supreme knowledge, and when we submit to His purpose, we are known of Him and walk with Him. As God says in **Isaiah 54:13**, *"All your children shall be taught by the LORD, and great shall be the peace of your children."*

*God says He will make us wiser than those who teach us, "You, through Your commandments, make me wiser than my enemies; for they are ever with me. I have more understanding than all my teachers, for Your testimonies are my meditation. I understand more than the ancients, because I keep Your precepts." (***Psalm 119:98-100***).*

I also remember God saying to Moses: "See, I have called by name Bezalel the son of Uri, the son of Hur, of the tribe of Judah. And I have filled him with the Spirit of God, in wisdom, in understanding, in knowledge, and in all manner of workmanship." **(Exodus 31:2-3)**.

We get to know God *"by first listening to God's Word with the help of the Holy Spirit. Second, we know God by thinking about His character as revealed in the Bible and the world. Third, we know God by obeying His commands. Finally, we know God through participating and service in His body, the church."* [17]

FINAL OVERVIEW

ARE YOU BETTER ABLE TO HANDLE FEAR?

- Acknowledging and accepting fear is necessary to triumph in this life.

- Preparing to deal with fear is equally important.

- The consequences or results arising from things we fear have to be considered—the 'what ifs.' What would you do if such a thing should happen?

- How would you continue to live?

- What if you should die today? Are you prepared?

- How will you enter eternity and how will you spend eternity?

- Will it be eternal punishment in hell or eternal joy in the presence of God?

HAVE YOU UNCOVERED PRIDE & FALSE HUMILITY?

How is your self-esteem?

Can you face egotism in your life?

Will you get to know God better and have His confidence?

Is your identity in God?

Do you look down on others?

Will you now seek more than ever to see and bring out the best in others?

ARE YOU WALKING IN THE LIGHT?

- God knows everything and walking with Him gives us access.

- Are you a child of God, a born-again believer with Jesus as your Savior?

- If not, may I invite you to consider making Him your Savior?

- Do you seek knowledge about things before you proceed on a project?

- Do you like to get advice on issues that you are not an expert in?

FOOTNOTES

Chapter 1

[1]   Gary R. Collins, 1988. "Christian Counseling" W Publishing Group. p. 77-78.

[2]   Gavin DeBecker, 1997. "The Gift of Fear." Little, Brown, and Company.

Chapter 2

[3]   Stokes and Lucas, 1988. "No Longer a Victim," p. 196.

[4]   Stokes & Lucas, p. 201.

Chapter 3

[5] Patrick Morley, 1997. "The Man in the Mirror," Zondervan, Grand Rapids, MI. pp. 261-262.

Chapter 4

[6] C. S. Lewis, 1996. "Mere Christianity," Touchstone, New York. p. 112.

[7] Al Hollingsworth, 1990. "Vertical Leap," B.O.S.S. The Movement.

[8] *Woodson, William. "History of Instrumental Music"; Kurfees, M.C. (1950), Instrumental Music in Worship.*

Chapter 5

[9] Patrick Morley, 1997. "The Man in the Mirror," p. 250.

Chapter 6

[10] Morris Sheats, 1996. "You Can Be Emotionally Healed," Christian Life Publication, Columbus, GA. p. 10.

Chapter 7

[11] Al Hollingsworth, 2000. "Vertical Leap," B.O.S.S. Global, Chino, CA. p. 25.

Chapter 8

12 C. S. Lewis, 1942. "The Screwtape Letters," Collins-Fontane, London, England, p. 9.

13 Gary Collins, 1988. "Christian Counseling," W Publishing Group, p. 563.

Chapter 9

14 J. I. Packer, 1973. "Knowing God," Intervarsity Press Downers Grove, IL, p. 23-26.

15 Rick Warren, 2002. "The Purpose Driven Life," Zondervan, Grand Rapids, MI, p. 18.

16 John Stott, 1958. "Basic Christianity," Inter-Varsity Press, Leicester, England, p. 8-9.

Chapter 10

17 Gary Collins, 1988. "Christian Counseling," W Publishing Group, p. 568.

Made in the USA
Middletown, DE
27 June 2018